READ AND SHARE™

The Story of Christmas

This book is for:

_____

From:

_____

Date:

_____

THE STORY OF CHRISTMAS
© 2007, 2009 by Thomas Nelson, Inc.

Previously published as part of *Read and Share™ Bible*.

Published in Nashville, Tennessee, by Thomas Nelson®. Thomas Nelson is a registered trademark of Thomas Nelson, Inc.

Thomas Nelson, Inc., books may be purchased in bulk for educational, business, fund-raising, or sales promotional use. For information, please e-mail SpecialMarkets@ThomasNelson.com.

Story based on *The Holy Bible, International Children's Bible*®, © 1986, 1988, 1999, 2005 by Thomas Nelson, Inc.

Story retold by Gwen Ellis.
Illustrated by Steve Smallman.

ISBN 978-1-4003-1457-7 (with DVD)
ISBN 978-1-4003-1468-3

Library of Congress Cataloging-in-Publication Data

Ellis, Gwen.
  The story of Christmas / retold by Gwen Ellis ; illustrated by Steve Smallman.
     p. cm.
  Includes bibliographical references and index.
  ISBN 978-1-4003-1468-3 (hardcover : alk. paper)
  1. Christmas—Juvenile literature. 2. Jesus Christ—Nativity—Juvenile literature.
I. Smallman, Steve. II. Title.
  BV45.E45 2009
  232.92—dc22

                                                      2009009228

Printed in China
07 08 09 10 11 WAI 5 4 3 2 1

READ AND SHARE™

The Story of Christmas

Retold by
Gwen Ellis

Illustrated by Steve Smallman

THOMAS NELSON
Since 1798

NASHVILLE   DALLAS   MEXICO CITY   RIO DE JANEIRO   BEIJING

An Angel's Message

Luke 1:5–20

A priest named Zechariah went to God's house to burn an incense offering. As soon as he was inside, the angel Gabriel appeared. "Zechariah, you and your wife, Elizabeth, will have a son. You will name him John," Gabriel said.

Zechariah didn't believe it was possible for Elizabeth and him to have a son. They were too old. "Because you don't believe me, Zechariah, you will not be able to talk until the baby is born," Gabriel said.

John was going to be a very important person. He would tell others to get ready because Jesus was coming.

A Baby Named John

Luke 1:57–66

Just as the angel Gabriel had said, a baby boy was born to Zechariah and his wife, Elizabeth.

Their friends were very happy for them. "Name him Zechariah after his father," they said. Zechariah still couldn't talk, so he wrote down, "His name is John." As soon as Zechariah wrote that, he could talk again.

His name is John.

People don't get to see angels very often, but when they do, they need to pay attention. Angels bring messages from God. What is another way God sends messages?

Mary's Big Surprise

Luke 1:26–38

Not long after his visit to Zechariah, the angel Gabriel went to see a young woman named Mary. She was a cousin to Elizabeth, Zechariah's wife. Mary lived in Nazareth and was engaged to marry Joseph, the carpenter.

"Don't be afraid, Mary," the angel said. "God is pleased with you. You will have a baby and will name Him Jesus. He will be called the Son of God." This was a big surprise to Mary.

What would you do if an angel suddenly appeared right here in front of you?

Joseph Marries Mary

Matthew 1:18–25

When Joseph heard the news that Mary was going to have a baby, he didn't know what to think. He wasn't married to her yet. God loved Joseph and wanted him to understand that the baby was from God and everything was going to be all right.

So God sent an angel to talk to Joseph in a dream. This angel told Joseph, "Name the baby Jesus. He will save people from their sins." When Joseph heard God's plan, he married Mary.

The name *Jesus* means "savior."
What does a savior do?

God's Baby Son

Luke 2:1–7

The ruler of the land, Augustus Caesar, made a new law to count all the people. Everyone had to register in their hometown. So Joseph and Mary went to their hometown, Bethlehem. The town was full of people. There was no place for Mary and Joseph to sleep.

Finally, Joseph found a place for them where the animals were kept. And that's where God's Baby Son was born. His first bed was on the hay in the box where the animals were fed.

Why do you think God would want His Son to be born where the animals were kept?

Some Sleepy Shepherds

Luke 2:8–12

That night, out in the fields, sleepy shepherds were taking care of their sheep. Suddenly an angel appeared in the sky. The angel's light was so bright, it hurt their eyes.

"Don't be afraid," the angel said. "I have good news for you. A baby was born in Bethlehem town tonight. He is your Savior. You will find Him lying in a feeding box."

Who was the first to hear about Baby Jesus?

What the Shepherds Saw

Luke 2:13–20

Then the whole sky filled
up with so many angels
no one could count them
all. They sang, "Glory
to God in heaven!"
And then, when the
song was over,
the angels
disappeared.

The shepherds hurried to Bethlehem. They found Mary and Joseph and saw Baby Jesus lying in the hay in the feeding box. The shepherds told them everything the angels had said about the child.

If you had been out there on the hill with the shepherds, what would you have been thinking when the angels left?

Gifts for Baby Jesus

Matthew 2:1–12

Soon many of the people who came to register in Bethlehem went home. Mary and Joseph moved into a house.

One day they had visitors who came from far away in the east. These visitors were wise men. They had followed a bright star to find little Jesus. They bowed down and worshiped God's only Son and gave Him expensive presents of gold, frankincense, and myrrh.

Why do you think the wise men came to see little Jesus?

Another Journey

Matthew 2:13–15

After the wise men left, God sent another angel to Joseph in a dream. "Take the child and Mary and go to Egypt," the angel said. "King Herod wants to kill Jesus. Stay in Egypt until I tell you it's safe to come home."

It was still night, but Joseph got up out
of bed and took Mary and Jesus and
headed for Egypt.

Joseph obeyed God immediately. And God kept his
family safe. Why is it good to obey quickly?

Home at Last!

Matthew 2:19–23

Mary, Joseph, and Jesus stayed in Egypt until God sent another angel to Joseph in a dream. "Get up and take Mary and Jesus and go home," said the angel. King Herod had died. He could never hurt them again. God and His angels had kept Mary, Joseph, and Jesus safe.

So with happy hearts, they went home
to live in Nazareth.

Whew! It was finally safe to go home. How do you
think Mary and Joseph felt about that?

Can You Retell the Story?

The pictures on this page and the next three pages are all mixed up. Do you remember what happened first? Point to the pictures in the correct order and retell the story.